MW00963358

SandCastle™

Character Concepts

Oh Behave!

Kelly Doudna

Consulting Editor, Diane Craig, M.A./Reading Specialist

ABDO
Publishing Company

Published by ABDO Publishing Company, 4940 Viking Drive, Edina, Minnesota 55435.

Copyright © 2007 by Abdo Consulting Group, Inc. International copyrights reserved in all countries. No part of this book may be reproduced in any form without written permission from the publisher. SandCastle™ is a trademark and logo of ABDO Publishing Company.

Printed in the United States.

Credits
Edited by: Pam Price
Curriculum Coordinator: Nancy Tuminelly
Cover and Interior Design and Production: Mighty Media
Photo Credits: AbleStock, BananaStock Ltd., Creatas, Hemera, ShutterStock, Stock Disc

Library of Congress Cataloging-in-Publication Data

Doudna, Kelly, 1963-
    Oh behave! / Kelly Doudna.
     p. cm. -- (Character concepts)
    ISBN-13: 978-1-59928-738-6
    ISBN-10: 1-59928-738-2
    1. Etiquette for children and teenagers. I. Title.

BJ1857.C5D67 2007
395.1'22--dc22

                                                              2006032285

SandCastle™ books are created by a professional team of educators, reading specialists, and content developers around five essential components—phonemic awareness, phonics, vocabulary, text comprehension, and fluency—to assist young readers as they develop reading skills and strategies and increase their general knowledge. All books are written, reviewed, and leveled for guided reading, early reading intervention, and Accelerated Reader® programs for use in shared, guided, and independent reading and writing activities to support a balanced approach to literacy instruction.

Let Us Know

SandCastle would like to hear your stories about reading this book. What is your favorite page? Was there something hard that you needed help with? Share the ups and downs of learning to read. We want to hear from you! To get posted on the ABDO Publishing Company Web site, send us e-mail at:

sandcastle@abdopublishing.com

SandCastle Level: Transitional

Oh Behave!*

Your character is a part of who you are. It is how you act when you go somewhere. It is how you get along with other people. It is even what you do when no one is looking!

You show character by being polite to people. You say please and thank you. You have good manners. You never accept a gift without saying thank you!

Jasmine's friend invited her to a sleepover. Jasmine is calling to let her friend know she'll be there. Jasmine has good manners.

Brandon's friends come to his summer party. He says hello to each of them as they arrive. Brandon has good manners.

Josh has a pizza party.
He makes sure that all
of his friends know each
other's names. Josh has
good manners.

Amber remembers to thank her friends for the gifts they brought. Amber has good manners.

Katie writes a thank-you note to each person who gave her a holiday gift. Katie has good manners.

Oh Behave!

Ella is invited
to a party
given by her
friend Kevin.
Ella sends a
note to say
she'll be there
right at seven.

Kevin opens the
door and says,
"Hello, how are you?"
Ella replies,
"I'm well, thank you.
How about you?"

Kevin says to Ella,
"This is my little
brother, Dave.
I hoped he
wouldn't be here,
but he promised
to behave."

When the party is over,
Ella tells Kevin
that she had fun.
She says, "Thank you
for inviting me,
but now I have to run!"

Did You Know?

President Thomas Jefferson is credited with making the handshake popular. It replaced bowing as the common way to greet another person.

Popular themes for birthday parties are sports, dinosaurs, and characters from movies and television.

The initials RSVP stand for the French phrase *répondez, s'il vous plaît*. It means "please reply." It is good manners to reply within a day or two of receiving an invitation.

Glossary

invite – to ask someone to do something or go somewhere with you.

manners – polite behavior.

promise – to give your word that you will do something.

sleepover – a party at which the guests spend the night. Also called a pajama party.

About SandCastle™

A professional team of educators, reading specialists, and content developers created the SandCastle™ series to support young readers as they develop reading skills and strategies and increase their general knowledge. The SandCastle™ series has four levels that correspond to early literacy development in young children. The levels are provided to help teachers and parents select appropriate books for young readers.

Emerging Readers
(no flags)

Beginning Readers
(1 flag)

Transitional Readers
(2 flags)

Fluent Readers
(3 flags)

These levels are meant only as a guide. All levels are subject to change.

To see a complete list of SandCastle™ books and other nonfiction titles from ABDO Publishing Company, visit **www.abdopublishing.com** or contact us at: 4940 Viking Drive, Edina, Minnesota 55435 • 1-800-800-1312 • fax: 1-952-831-1632